Reveal the
of Graph
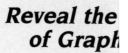

Reveal the Secrets of Graphology

Gilbert Oakley

Edited and with a Foreword by
Patricia Marne

W. Foulsham & Co. Ltd.
London • New York • Toronto • Cape Town
Sydney

W. Foulsham & Company Limited
Yeovil Road, Slough, Berkshire, SL1 4JH

ISBN 0–572–01422–8

Printed in Great Britain at
St Edmunsbury Press, Bury St Edmunds.

Contents

Foreword

Patricia Marne

Founder Member and Chairwoman,
The Graphology Society

In view of the rapidly increasing interest in graphology in Britain and elsewhere recently, this book provides an excellent guide to the basic characteristics of handwriting analysis and serves to demonstrate the writer's skill in showing the individual traits that can be revealed in a few lines of script.

It has something for the student graphologist and can act as a refresher for the more advanced reader. A most important fact is the accuracy of the text. This writer has studied his subject for many years and his grasp of the individual nature of handwriting is expressed in the clarity of his explanations and illustrations. His observation and interpretations of the varying types of handwriting characteristics shown in this book constitute useful graphological knowledge, particularly for the beginner who wishes to take up this fascinating science.

Preface

Would you like to be able to determine the character and mental attitude of those people who mean the most to you in your life by understanding the significance of their handwriting? Without them knowing?

If you employ people, it would be handy to know their potential before you signed them up. Or to know exactly what your boss is like—deep down under his façade of professionalism.

Falling in love is an easy job. It happens to all of us all the time. It would be useful to be able to delve beneath the surface; to know the true character lurking beneath the glamour.

If you have a big money deal coming off, how nice to know whether you can really trust the person or persons with whom you have dealings.

As a parent, your children's friends of both sexes could be summed-up in a tactful manner and no-one would be any the wiser! Except yourself.

Letters from relatives and friends, from chance acquaintances, could take on new meaning. A glance at the envelope of a letter addressed to someone else could give you an idea of its contents.

The subconscious wishes, hopes, ambitions, repressions and frustrations of those nearest and dearest could be laid bare to you. You would be able to detect signs and symptoms of ill health, mental and emotional crises. Perhaps be able to step in, in time, and save future complications.

People would look upon you with new respect. Bring their problems to you—and those of their friends and relatives.

And what of yourself?

At last you would be able to know the true 'you'. And to take urgent steps to correct things in character-formation that were doubtful. You would have your eyes opened to those little things below the surface of which others were aware but that you little suspected. You could turn yourself into a far more likeable personality—once you knew exactly where you were going wrong.

As to career, there would be opportunities to discover whether you were following the right vocation. Whether figure work really was for you. What artistic and creative abilities you possess. All these vitally important things would be revealed to you by knowledge of the amazing power of your pen.

Of all 'ologys' and 'isms', graphology—the science of character-reading by handwriting—is one of the most reliable. Used by police departments the world over, offered as evidence at famous criminal trials, the power of the pen has been found mightier than the sword.

Handwriting has, as its source, the delicate nervous system which faithfully records attitudes of mind arising from character and philosophy towards life. If character changes, so also does the handwriting of the individual.

But dominant characteristics of the writing remain, never to change, however much the writer might try to adopt a 'new style' of writing. If a person develops a new set of attitudes to life, his handwriting remains essentially the same.

The trained graphologist observes this. Now you can have an opportunity to do the same.

Further—you will be able to set new behaviour-patterns for yourself, based on the things you will learn about yourself. You will be able to direct your present and future moves in your choice of associates, friends, love and marriage partners.

Eventually, if you diligently study this book, you will discover insight. You will be able to analyse the contents of letters, the significance of signatures, interpret pen pictures in 'doodles' and the twists and turns of loops and downstrokes.

New attitudes, new philosophies, movements such as Existentalism, the re-birth of old schools of thought in music, painting, fashion, literature— all show their influences in present-day scripts. In turn, these changes indicate a variety of new façets of character formation and mind development.

The ability to analyse character is to be successful, happy and healthy; to draw around you the very best and the most reliable friends; to make the most of your love life.

The character analyses in these pages will open your eyes to yourself, give you amazing insight into your friends and relations.

Forewarned is forearmed!

Gilbert Oakley

PART 1

Living and Working with People—How to Pick the Right Friends, Partners and Colleagues

CHAPTER 1

Learning to Write

From an early age, parents, brothers, sisters, relatives, friends and teachers try to influence a child's mind on the important question of how the child shall write.

Before the mysteries of language are introduced to the child, it has to learn how to form its letters so that it can build words and sentences and phrases in order to interpret the language of the country to which it belongs.

This is often a rather long and sometimes painful process, both to the child and to all those interested in its education.

A great point that parents, teachers and those interested in the formation of a child's handwriting sometimes fail to recognise or to accept is the fact that, once the child is born, it brings into the world an inborn anticipation of the sort of handwriting its kind of character will inevitably adopt. That is a basic fact that neither science nor society will successfully challenge. Neither will they ever be able to interfere with it.

Character and personality potential are born with the child, as surely as it is born with fingers and toes, a head and arms. And these characteristics and personality façets it inherits from its parents, its grandparents and from way back among its ancestors.

The task of the parent is to smooth the way for the eventual teacher or tutor who will have the final task of teaching the child to write legibly. But there is one thing that neither parent nor teacher will ever influence or eradicate, and that is the dominant, pre-conceived characteristics that are there—at the moment of birth—and that, later in life, the child will adopt as photographs of its mind, its inherited tendencies, its character, personality and general attitude towards life.

There are so many different styles of handwriting. As, indeed, there are so many different character façets in human nature. There is an accepted formula for the formation of letters of the alphabet and every child learns this formula.

It is, however, the child's particular and individual interpretation of this formula that causes confusion in the minds of parents and teachers in the early formative years of the child's life. It is the interpretation that is challenged by these people who seek to make the child write as they write.

Instinctively, the child—seeking to portray its mind in its play with pen and pencil—resists this domination, knowing inwardly, though of course unconsciously, that its attempts at self-expression are being thwarted and frustrated.

Confusion now comes on the scene as the child attempts to do as it is told and to form its letters and words in the ways dictated by its parents and teachers. It is willing to learn the basic rules of writing and usually makes a good job of so doing. But, struggling under the surface most of the time is the insistent urge to express itself in the way in which it feels compelled to do.

That is why so many children, for so long, write so badly. They are struggling to learn how to form their letters, trying to form them as daddy or mummy or teacher wants them to be formed. At the same time, they are trying to let their egos thrust through and to form their letters in the way they—and the promptings of their developing characters—dictate they should be formed.

It is seldom until they reach their late teens they are allowed, by teachers, to develop their own style. And this is the time when character is developing in earnest, that their handwriting settles down into what it is going to be for the rest of their lives.

But one interesting thing is that, from a comparatively early age, certain characteristics become predominant in their handwriting and persist throughout their lives. It is these dominant characteristics for which the trained graphologist looks when analysing the character of the writer.

However much the writer may seek to change the style of his handwriting, these dominant characteristics will remain and will never be truly disguised.

These show through in the written word like touch in piano-playing, technique in painting, craftsmanship in sculpting, carpentering and all creative outlets. They all establish the character of the individual, and can never be changed in basic manifestations.

Forgers are caught out because the dominant characteristics of their handwriting assert themselves, subconsciously, in the facsimile the forger makes of another's handwriting. Poison-pen letter writers who print their stuff come unstuck because they forget to exclude those little quirks, twists and twirls that characterise their own handwriting.

Handwriting is, indeed, the true mirror of the soul. The really reliable indication of character, personality and attitude towards life.

In no way, though, can the future be foretold by an individual's handwriting. Character, temperament, abilities and tendencies are shown, later to be recognised and nurtured and made to fit the individual's pattern for the future.

Weaknesses of character can be checked with resulting good effects later in life.

Everything one does in life can be subconsciously portrayed in doodling, pen pictures, the way in which an envelope is addressed, a signature is made, initials are formed, figures are drawn, lines are ruled, margins are decided, letters, words, phrases and sentences are formed by the pen in the writer's hand.

The brain sends a message to the hand that holds the pen. The pen translates this message into loops and curves, circles, strokes, dashes and dots. These form letters and words that stand for sounds that establish human communications. But the message sent from the brain to the hand that holds the pen determines the thought behind the interpretation of that message in the form of symbols. It is the form that is the photograph of the person.

CHAPTER 2

The Formative Years

Seven years of age is the age of reason when a child begins to form attitudes and ideas about itself and life in general.

Now, the pen, pencil and paint brush begin to be important tools with which it can begin to express itself. In the child's pictures of its parents, brothers, sisters, friends and teachers, in its conception of cows in a field, houses, ships at sea and the thousand and one little pictures it loves to draw and paint can be seen the intelligent mind striving for recognition and individuality.

This becomes particularly apparent in the child's handwriting which it now begins to use as a favourite mode of projecting its personality.

This formative process continues until the boy or girl has reached the age of fourteen. Life moves forward in cycles of about seven years and it is really quite remarkable how an individual's outlook, abilities and capabilities do take forward strides as each seven-year-cycle develops.

By fourteen years of age, the child has developed decided characteristics which begin to show in his handwriting.

If he is frank and honest, this begins to show in the way in which he opens and closes his small 'a' and 'o'. His ambition-drive can be seen in the way in which he crosses his 't'. In a thousand and one little ways he will begin to show the type of person he is going to grow up to be.

From fourteen years to eighteen or twenty-one is the next cycle of character development. Puberty is well under way, the child is changing over from the bisexual and homosexual stages to the normal heterosexual stage. A code of morals is developing. A standard of living is beginning to implant itself on the adolescent mind. Now one can look for more decisive downstrokes to letters in words. The signature begins to take on force and individuality. Every time the adolescent signs his or her name, the signature contains within itself a pen picture of what this person aspires to be—the sort of stamp he or she wants to make on the world.

A signature says: 'Well, here I am. This is me'. A signature is all its name implies—it is the final word that sums up the personality behind it.

From twenty-one to twenty-eight the individual now takes his or her place in life and becomes really adult and mature. The handwriting takes on a firm appearance. Strokes are decisive, deliberate, calculated and precise. The writer is now a mature adult.

From twenty-eight onwards, through the rest of life's seven-year cycles, the handwriting remains basically the same. The realisation of ambitions may give more flamboyancy to the capital letters, or perhaps lend more strength to the signature. Downstrokes may get more emphatic. The writer tells the world, 'I am here. I have made it'.

Until old age sets in and the hand becomes quavery and weak, handwriting will be recognisable as the particular 'hand' of such-and-such a person. Even in extreme old age, the time-worn characteristics will remain.

The reverse side of the picture will, of course, show 'reverses' in life. Instead of realising ambition, the person may be a failure. There is illness, frustration, disappointment. There is a deviation of the sex drive that will show itself in an alteration of certain formations of letters and words. But throughout, dominant characteristics will remain and the handwriting will be basically and essentially the same.

With reversal of circumstances, with failure and a general downward trend in life, the signature can begin to show lack of emphasis and conviction. Compared with earlier signatures when the writer was successful, or determined to be successful, much life may have gone out of the signature, illustrating the onset of inferiority and the lack of cocksureness that before showed through so emphatically.

The same may be said for 'figure work'. Confidence in present financial affairs leads the writer to form his figures with a flourish. There is pride in writing cheques, tallying figures in the cash books and so on. But when things tend to get bad the writer will diminish the physical size of the figures in the accounts and on the cheques. He does this as a result of a subconscious desire to hide them from the enquiring world, not to admit to their worrisome and embarrassing presence in life.

Handwriting is almost as reliable as the science of fingerprints when it comes to identifying people. No two sets of handwriting are exactly the same, although similar characteristics do, of course, show through in specimens of many people. Nevertheless, there is always just that little variance in the presentation of similar characteristics that make them the property of the individual writer.

It is these little variances that the forger will seek to hide but will very seldom succeed in hiding from the astute eye of the trained graphologist.

In a similar way, the trained graphologist will be able to detect characteristic signs that conform to set standards handed down for many years where the study of handwriting is concerned. These set standards of characteristics and what they mean have been sifted so carefully and comparisons made in so many cases that it has become patent these characteristics can safely be applied to certain personality and character traits to be found in individuals in general.

Things do not end with just the formation of letters and words. The seven-year-cycles produce variations in the forward or the backward slope of a person's handwriting. They can reveal alterations in their habits of wide margins at the right and left hand side of the paper on which they are writing; in the way in which they connect or disconnect, with unfailing regularity, the letters in the words they form; in the regularity or irregularity in which they write in straight or crooked lines; in the way in which, when they write on guide lines on lined notepaper, they keep to the lines or rise and fall above and below them at regular intervals.

The first example shows an erratic and unreliable character, whereas the second shows steadiness and ambition.

CHAPTER 3

How Knowledge of Handwriting Secrets Can Help You Find Happiness

What benefits will you obtain from learning how to read character from handwriting?

Everyone is, instinctively, adept at learning to recognise the handwriting of people known to them. A glance at the envelope and they will be able to say, 'This letter is from So-and-So'.

But how much nicer (and more advantageous) also to be able to say, after looking at the envelope (and before opening it), 'So-and-So has some good or bad news in this letter'. Or to be able to see in the letter character façets previously unknown to you.

In addition, how useful, if you are an employer, to be able to assess the potential of a prospective employee on first reading the letter of application for a position with your firm.

Conversely, how nice to get a letter from a prospective employer and to be able to evaluate his potential before you sign up with him!

Again, socially, you could become most popular with your set if you are able to delineate the handwriting of your friends, their families and business acquaintances.

Expert knowledge we can possess that is denied others, provided it is knowledge for good, is always useful to acquire. Knowledge of the secrets contained in the handwriting of all those with whom you deal can bring great happiness, a far greater insight into their characters and can, assuredly, help you to plan your future better by being forewarned.

Better friendships will be formed if you know what sort of people you are dealing with.

You may think that once you have learnt what your handwriting reveals about your character, you will be able to change your character! That of course will be impossible. However, you will certainly be able to correct little faults of character development that you see revealed in your handwriting and thereby improve your position socially, within the family and in regard to your business life.

It is never too late in life to re-adjust one's temperament for the good and to dismiss permanently annoying character traits seen in you by others but, at the moment, unknown to you.

Make no mistake, though, if a sudden and concentrated study of your handwriting makes you aware that your hand is not a very good one, and you seek to change it, you may succeed up to a point but you will most certainly not change the inbred, characteristic and subconscious nature of your hand. Even if you succeed in changing your hand drastically, switch from sloping to the right to sloping to backhand, or start to spread your letters out more, or to elongate them, or to join them continuously or to separate certain letters in words, you will still keep to your own, individual style. That style is a personal photograph of you.

Because I think a great deal about you

Because I think a great deal about you

The same characteristic heavy up- and down-strokes are maintained in these two samples, although the writer changes the slope of his hand.

CHAPTER 4

Are These Your Friends or Enemies?

Meeting people is something we do all the time. Decisions have sometimes to be made on the spot before one is aware of the type of person with whom one is dealing.

However, when correspondence arises between you and the new friend or acquaintance, you will be able to use your new knowledge to assess character potential and to know the sort of person or persons with whom you are dealing.

that you are

This example shows a firm, energetic script with a nice rightward slant indicating an outward-going social attitude.

.the most interesting

This second sample shows a thin script revealing a highly sensitive nature and a lack of reserve energy to fall back on. This person is a touchy individual, quick to react to slights, whether real or imagined.

Here, below, are three different types of handwriting that might well please you were you to see them in the letters written to you by your old or new friends.

They show thrift, a far-seeing nature and the ability to be a good salesman which means strength of character, drive and determination.

Early days yet in which to

The first line of handwriting is unusual in that most letters are joined to the other in a calculated manner, as if the writer was not only weighing up every word but every letter as he wrote! This shows great attention to detail, a precise way of looking at life and a good head for business. The determined, thick interpretation of the capital 'E' speaks of strength of purpose; a subconscious betrayal of a convinced ego. The looped downstrokes to the 'y' show flamboyance but a preconceived ability to deal with problems in the quickest, most inexpensive and simplest way possible.

Early days yet

The second specimen is crudely heavy, but shows firmness of character and great resolve and purpose in life. Intuition is strongly marked, as also is a decided flair for inspiration and on-the-spot decision. This handwriter may be a bit difficult to get on with. A strongly shown artistic and creative outlook might make for temperament but a certain sense of generosity would, no doubt, compensate for any difficult emotional habits.

.Early days yet in

The third example of handwriting is level headed. It is that of a persuasive personality but not a plausible person. Straight dealings can be expected from such an individual but a scatty, rather irresponsible sense of humour may make such a person an embarrassment at times. Ambition is shown in the strokes to the 'i', and the stroke on the 't' shows a day dreamer with ability to realise day dreams.

These specimens have, of course, many variations. You may see a hand that is similar in some respects but which differs in other ways. Look, however, for a dominating similarity all round and it should be an easy job to determine who may be made into a firm, reliable friend, or who might well turn out to be an enemy—at least to your peace of mind!

CHAPTER 5

How to Recognise Sincerity

Sincere friends are what most of us seek in our social and business fields.

It may be that, in the past, with vague feelings that handwriting does mean something as far as character is concerned, we have thought that an upright, firm, easily-readable hand denotes sincerity. That such a person writing in such a way is bound to be sincere, reliable, trustworthy.

The opposite, in many cases, is the truth. The too-careful writer is giving too much thought to the impression he is likely to make on others. He may be a slow-thinker, perhaps, or calculating to a mischievous degree.

The erratic writer, the all-over-the-paper writer, is often generous, kind, patient, tolerant. His handwriting portrays his attitude to life: an all-embracing acceptance of humanity in general. No cool, calculated scheming here. Write—and tell the world!

Here are three samples of handwriting showing dependability, trustworthiness and strength of mind. Three valuable characteristics we all like to think we possess and certainly hope most of our closest friends and colleagues possess.

Yours Ever, Seymour

The first specimen is humorous. See the emphatic downstroke right through the 's'. Not really necessary, but a little refinement the writer could not resist! The capital 'E' is grossly exaggerated, again illustrating a great sense of fun. People with a sense of fun usually have also a great sense of responsibility and are reliable. So this writer is likely to treat everything as a huge joke, but when up against a crisis is likely to come out tops. The pointed characters to the letters shows a sharp mind, quick on the uptake. This again points to reliability. The writing slopes upwards in an ambitious curve. Not a writer likely to let you down!

Yes... by all means let me have

The second handwriting example is that of a trustworthy person, heavy-handed, likely to be a bit dictatorial and to have a tendency to lay down the law. But, at rock bottom, a firm character. There is slight hesitancy shown that might reveal itself in making decisions but this would spring from a sense of caution rather than from an undecided mind.

The Greek-style small 'e' in 'yes' shows a scholastic turn of mind. Good breeding might well be here, certainly intellect and intelligence. There is a tendency for the word 'the' to appear to be a bit top heavy. This shows the writer is likely to reach the brink of an emotional precipice and to teter on the edge, undecided as to what to do for the best. His judgement would be correct in the long run, however, as evinced by his blunt, powerful up-strokes to the letters 'l', 't' and 'h'.

Have you ever paused to think

Now, in the third specimen, there is a squarish hand here that shows the individual right away. Eccentric, possibly, but a person with great strength of mind. Someone who knows where he or she is going, and who is likely to get there in the shortest time possible by the shortest route. A certain childish outlook is retained, however, a throwover from younger days. But this is the law of reversed effort in action. The writer, intellec-tual, with a considerable capacity for taking pains, relieves him or herself from time to time with juvenile wishful thinking and pleasant, immature day dreams. Such a hand, read on first sight, might well give the impression of being unformed, that the writer was not fully developed emotionally or mentally. This, however, would be incorrect. Maturity shows through in almost every stroke. The childishness of the character formation of the letters is more a subconscious subterfuge than anything else, and more for the amusement of the

writer than a deliberate attempt to mislead. This is
a sign of the eccentric side of the writer.

Depend on me to do my lovel best for you!

Here is a sincere hand. Simple, a little immature perhaps, but written by a trustworthy adult.

CHAPTER 6

Test for the Emotional Stability of Your Friends

Emotional stability means that a person has reached mental maturity either through age or through experience or both.

Emotional stability is most important when it is examined in the light of engaged couples with an eye to a happy or not-so-happy future together.

My Dear Tim, I write to thank you for your kindness in letting me know, in such good time, of your decisions for

This is a specimen of a letter written by a man whose continuity of thought shown in the way he links his letters together is proof of his emotional stability. There is an even flow in his writing that, although it leaves something to be desired as far as legibility is concerned, gives a complete picture of directness of vision, an 'I-know-where-I'm-going' outlook and courage of convictions. Strokes to the letter 't' are, generally, long and generous, running through other letters that follow. This shows he is all-embracing in his attitude towards people

33

and is likely to take everything into account in his dealings with them. It indicates a sort of protective cloak he is ready to throw over those whom he likes the most. The small capital 'T' in the first line shows modesty that allows for accomplishment without trumpet-blowing.

Can make of my handwriting

The second example of handwriting also indicates emotional balance and stability insomuch as the writing is all on the level, letters are well joined and there is little or no exaggeration to the capitals. The loops to the rear of the upstroke of the letter 'd' indicate the ability to delve into the past for inspiration for the present and for the future. A balanced sense of humour is seen in the way in which the 'i' is dotted. A sense of values and a gift for getting things in their right perspective and proportion can be seen in the firm stroke on the letter 't'; not too high up to show the day-dreamer mentality nor too low to indicate depression and melancholia. It is a well balanced hand which to shows a realist and a thoroughly practical person.

CHAPTER 7

Good for Long-Term Love and Marriage?

Love letters are exchanged in their millions every day. Extravagant phrases and flowery speeches give no true indication whatsoever as to the character of the love-sick writers involved!

How handy, though, for the wondering woman to be able to see at a glance whether or not her suitor is a man of character and good intentions! And good for the man, also, to know whether the girl he is pursuing is worth the trouble!

Every specimen of handwriting in this book showing good or bad characteristics may be avidly examined and diligently applied by the man or woman in love as a secret test of future hopes.

Here is a specimen of handwriting that could equally have been written by a man or a woman that shows a practical and a generous person. Attributes much to be desired in a partner.

and I think it extremely kind of you to give me such a splendid mention. Perhaps we can meet soon?

The angular character to the letters shows intellect. Precise dots to the 'i' shows painstaking deliberation and an aptitude to thoroughness. The writer is a hobby-lover, domesticated. Rather an involved nature could mean much fun provided the parties did not allow themselves to become too involved in matters too deep for them. The up-and-down nature of the writing is a sign of indulgence and kindliness, useful traits in any relationship. The angles will manifest themselves in the practical handyman-or-woman theme. A simple outlook on life, taking it as a whole, is indicated and this, in the long run, is likely to overcome the involved nature that will, from time to time, creep through. Letter 'o' is well closed in showing a frank and truthful nature. Generally a well-formed, lucid hand portrays the home-loving personality, someone with a sense of thrift plus a generous nature when required. The specimen shown reveals these attributes in spite of the fact that the lettering appears, on first sight, to be that of a rather formidable human being!

CHAPTER 8

A Realist and a Head-in-the-Air Type

You are either down-to-earth and a realist, or you are a head-in-the-air type.

Life is sometimes hard for the realist because, by nature, he feels compelled to face up to the hard things in human existence and has not the sometimes-useful capacity for burying his head in the sand and avoiding (or not accepting) trouble.

For the idealist, the head-in-the-air type, life can, sometimes, be a merry doddle. Until he is found out and his day dreams are exploded, and he finds himself having to come down to earth with a bump!

Trust the realist. You will have a hard time with him, on and off. But things will always be in their proper perspective.

Amuse yourself with the idealist. But dilly-dally only for a short while, for there will be trouble in the long run.

Here are some specimens of handwriting from the realist and the idealist. And, no doubt, you will be surprised to see that the realist has a hand you would probably concede the idealist—and vice-versa.

Explanation?

The realist, sure of himself, can lend a fluency to his handwriting that the idealist by reason of his subconscious knowledge that he is, after all, only day dreaming through life cannot give his handwriting. He must go carefully and cautiously. For, as he writes, he shows the innermost fears and misgivings of his subconscious life—so very far removed from his conscious, unrealistic, idealist existence.

Remember I will always ȝole for

This first specimen belongs to the realist. It is not easy to read. It flows on with a boldness and an abandon, but it betrays the happy spirit. This is a mature writer. Mature in mind, not necessarily in physical years. With maturity goes honesty as well. A realist is automatically honest. Letters are linked, showing continuity of thought and great powers of concentration. Letters are sharply formed, showing keen observation and an aptitude to look at life through a sophisticated eye. The 'o' is closed well at the top. This is honesty. The upstrokes to the letter are not high or exaggerated. This shows a level of constructive thinking that does not soar above the rational. The capital 'R' is large and generous.

Beautiful though you may be, never forget that

The second specimen flows easily but there is a sense of effort in the formation of the letters. The writer writes deliberately, forcing his hand forward with every letter, conscious of the effort it is to live in a perpetual day dream. This hand, though, looks better formed than the first specimen. It is more legible and seems to illustrate a far stronger character. That, of course, is not so. Here, also, is a person who might well be sexually unbalanced. Or at least, a person who is inclined to deviate from the normal. That is shown by the extreme heaviness of the handwriting and by a certain viciousness in the way the pen seems to stab into the paper. But an idealist, you would say, could hardly be sexually aberrated? Surely such a person would be idealistic about sex, of all things, looking upon it as a spiritual rather than as a physical function? It is a fact that idealism, in some cases, is akin to sensualism. That sex is used as an escape from reality and as a cloak for outlooks and attitudes in this direction that are distinctly inverted. See a kind of cringing theme in the way in which the letters, including the small 't', are all about the same size. There appears to be a reluctance to rise above things, to assert the ego. And this might well be so, for the idealist, eager to assert the ego in a world of realists, generally finds it hard going!

Actually — I never behave myself at a party!

This example illustrates the real 'head-in-the-air' type. He loves attention.

CHAPTER 9

Would This Person Make a Good Worker?

Employers often find it hard to assess the potential of a prospective employee on first sight and face value. Conversation at the first interview no doubt produces many valuable impressions. The first letter of application for a situation the employer gets, gives immediately an idea of the kind of person the applicant is. At least it does to the unversed employer who, of course, is not a graphologist, trained or otherwise.

Naturally the first letter of application in reply to an advertisement, or whatever it is that has led the applicant to write in, is, without any doubt at all, a splendid guide for the employer. Provided he understands graphology and can deleniate character. But few bosses can.

There follow two samples of handwriting and these may be taken as fairly representative of good and bad characteristics showing through, but, of course, all the specimens of handwriting and their analyses must be applied if a thorough test of character is being made by the careful employer.

The very essence of successful life does not apply

Although this first specimen seems to be a rather careless hand, there is, however, method in the seeming madness. This is the handwriting of a good worker, a conscientious individual, a vigorous go-ahead type who brooks no interference and knows precisely where he or she is going. Legibility is not necessarily an indication of good character. Sometimes the clear hand betrays a cunning and a deliberation that can lead to bad things. There is a strongly marked sense of humour in this hand, something that will carry the writer through many a bad patch.

But I am afraid I will never be the sort of person to

The second example of handwriting, with its untidy and sensual downstrokes indicates the disordered, untidy, unmethodical mind; the unreliable fellow. Weakness of character shows in the fainter lettering, and impulsiveness and untrustworthiness are shown in the sudden but very regular reversion to the heavy strokes—that is a suddenly rising temper, almost uncontrolled. There is no sense of fun shown in this hand at all. The writer is cringing, and could well be a parasite. This is certainly not an ambitious hand. There is little foresight indicated, and the writer is content to live for today and to hell with tomorrow.

The handwriting of potential employees varies insomuch as it is little to no indication of mental age, at least that is the main point put forward in a census of opinion carried out among a few hundred business executives in Great Britain recently. On average, the cleverest and most promising employees had a certain strength and maturity in their handwriting that showed immediately their ability to shoulder responsibility and to delegate authority.

CHAPTER 10

This is a Signature You Can Trust

When a prospective employee gets a letter from a man or woman who is to be a prospective employer, the signature is an all-important indication of what things there may be to come.

Yours Sincerely

John Hamilton

Here is a pleasant enough hand showing promise of a warm heart, a tendency to look back instead of being too forward-thinking and a strongly marked sense of humour. There are other specimens of signatures later on in the book, but this example shows at a glance a kindly, good business man with a generous disposition. The capital letters to his name are not too exaggerated, therefore he does not have too high an opinion of himself and is not likely to project his ego to the detriment of happy associations with his employees.

maybe the next time you

Here is a small, mean, cramped hand, showing thrift carried to excess. The writer does not have a good business head. He is something of a slave driver and not likely to be a very good payer. Absence of a dot to the 'i' shows absent-mindedness and general slackness. Such an individual would be unreliable, have a prying as opposed to an enquiring mind and would not be very good company. There is no marked aptitude for his work, whatever it might be, neither are there indications of ambition. This would not bode well for prospects of advancement for an employee.

This is the signature of a shy and introverted man who shys away from people.

This signature you can trust. The generous formation of letters shows an open mind. The right slant shows sociability, the quick writing indicates perception and spontaneity.

CHAPTER 11

The Spoken Word and the Written Word

Calligraphy is the art of writing. Everybody writes so everybody is a calligraphist. Graphology is the art of discovering character from handwriting. Not everyone is a graphologist.

Everybody has character, be it good or bad.

A thought starts in the mind. If the thinker wishes to share it with those around him, he requires some form of understandable translation. Thought translation is possible in two forms. In the spoken word or in the written word.

Spoken words are later, in some cases, committed to paper. Written words are read. Mental attitude towards the thought under review is illustrated by delivery, voice projection, inflexion and intonation. The speaker shows what he thinks about the thought in the way in which he translates the thought into the spoken word.

The writer does not necessarily show what he thinks about the dominant thought as he writes it down, but he does show what his general character and mental attitude is. Therefore the wise graphologist can more or less determine his general attitude towards the thoughts now expressed on paper.

So, if a man with a generous nature records his thoughts about money in the written word, one can trace genuineness and sincerity in all subjects written about dealing with finance. On the other hand, the mean-natured individual will show traces of his failings throughout his script.

CHAPTER 12

Four Types of Handwriting Style

The following examples show four types of hand-writing styles: arcade, garland, thread and angular. The letters 'm' and 'n' are the clues to look for to determine the various types of script.

analyse more than

Arcade handwriting shows a secret nature, reserved and often introspective. When the arcades are made with high arches they may indicate musical or artistic talent.

writing with reference

Garland writing is basically non-aggressive script, rather rounded and shallow, with upturned arcades. It is sometimes referred to a feminine script and does appear more often in female handwriting than male.

Take my writing.

Thread handwriting, with its sinuous curves, shows a strong urge for manipulation. The writer is able to extricate himself from difficult situations with ease and usually possesses considerable psychological talent for dealing with people to his own advantage. Hard to pin down, these writers rarely give away their motivations.

now is the time

Angular script belongs to the more aggressive and dominant personality who will not mind using force if necessary. The head rules the heart, and there is an inbuilt defensiveness in the angular writer's personality which makes him calculating.

CHAPTER 13

States of Mind and Negative Attitudes

More than anything else, mental attitude shows in a person's handwriting.

While no strength of mind or character will eradicate signs of ill-health in handwriting, so no effort of will, however strong, will hide weak character indications in handwriting. Below are specimens of handwriting showing tendencies to states of mind and attitudes. Once again they are not to be taken as standard, but as examples of your friends' writing who are suspected of suffering from similar character traits, attitudes and states of mind, and they will show interesting parallels.

try to do your best for me

The inferiority complex hand.

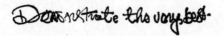

The neurotic hand.

Active people

The over-emotional hand.

try a little patience

The eccentric hand.

really, dear, you must try

The sexually ambiguous hand.

and as far as I can see

The sexually immature hand.

begin to try to see my point of

The impotent hand.

I was very pleased to hear

The frigid hand.

You are more

This hand shows immaturity.

The perfect

This hand shows sensuality.

C'mne home

This hand shows aggressiveness.

Over and

This hand shows deceitfulness.

Monahd Eiii doall I

This hand shows the masochist.

The mind is actively at work when forming upstrokes and downstrokes, loops, curls, ascending and descending lines, backhand and forward-sloping lettering. Here are some specimens of thoughts betrayed in handwriting.

maybe graphology

Copybook handwriting. Dull, a plodder.

Death and

Showing a sense of form and design.

Perhaps

This hand shows a sexual hang-up.

Try a joyful

An artistic, musical hand.

much travelling

An easy-going, tolerant hand.

Many men

A hand showing manual skill.

Boastful

A boastful, vain hand.

Going away soon!

A person who likes a firm foundation.

hoped to get something

A person who aims high, but lacks an intellectual mind.

CHAPTER 14

The Fascination of Exaggerated Capitals

Capital letters are fascinating to some writers. Many people use capitals in the middle of their writing, so great is the fascination for using them. This is not an indication of lack of knowledge, but is the ego asserting itself.

The decisive capital.

The show-off capital.

The precise capital.

The artistic capital.

The inferiority capital.

The resolute capital.

The obstinate capital.

The exhibitionist capital.

Mechanical skill.

Vanity, self love.

Intelligence, good taste.

Shrewd, calculating.

Lives in the past.

A sexual quirk.

Wasteful, extravagant.

Flamboyant, seeks attention.

Strong mother influence.

PART 2

Expressions of Human Sensitivity

CHAPTER 15

Occupational Symbols

People of some intelligence who specialise in a particular job, and very often this is a creative job, are prone to weave occupational symbols into their handwriting. It is not difficult for the trained graphologist to see what is the dominant interest in a man or woman's life from a study of this particular sort of grapho-symbolism.

People who follow creative bents or whose jobs are creative in themselves are in many cases what one could call 'spoilt' artists insomuch as they wish they could paint or draw but cannot. The composer or the musician, for instance, would love to interpret his art in terms of form, line and mass.

But music has to be written and played. It cannot be portrayed in paint or in charcoal. Therefore, the musician or composer unconsciously uses his or her handwriting as a medium for this frustrated self-expression.

The same may also be said for the romanticist, the idealist, the philosopher and so on. The artist, of course, with a canvas of his own and paints to go with it, is more fortunate. Nevertheless he will also use pen, pencil and paper to continue the projection of himself as an artist and he will also use the occupational symbolism in all he writes.

Basically, the pen in the hand of the average man and woman is the brush in the unconscious creative worker's hand, and the paper is his canvas.

Here are some examples of occupational symbolism evinced in handwriting. These may be looked for in the the handwriting of friends you know well. Even if their jobs are humdrum and uncreative, far removed from anything artistic, they may pursue artistic hobbies, have artistic and creative outlets. On the other hand they may be completely frustrated and repressed in these directions and may not have the slightest aptitude for translating their creative urges into proper, material forms. They will, however, carry these dreams over into their handwriting.

Some people, could, in later life, discover a hidden talent and start to make use of it either in their daily jobs or most certainly as hobbies or spare-time occupations.

Yng a little

Varying sizes can show an erratic personality,

Because you

or an original thinker, an artistic person.

many of the ways

A connected script shows a systematic worker.

and suddenly you began to tell me

Disconnected script shows an ideas person.

find me a

The use of the money symbol shows a mercenary mind.

Retribution will follow

Exaggeration shows the egotist, full of personal vanity.

Take a steady trip down the

High 't' strokes: this is the idealist and shows a lack of reality.

Fancy free and

This is the childish romantic.

try not to hesitate if

This is the stubborn, opinionated person, using the thick 't' bar.

Also all too a long trip to the soil

This person is moody and unpredictable, shown by the erratic slant.

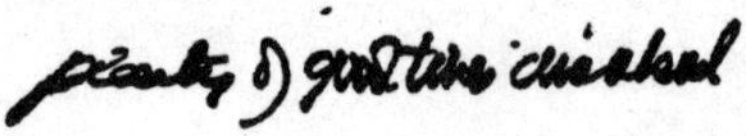

[handwritten: penalty of greatness checked]

The downward slope indicates the pessimist.

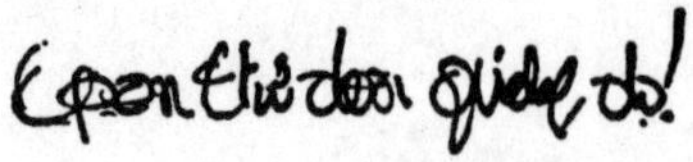

[handwritten: Open the door quick oh!]

This original script indicates someone with a sense of humour.

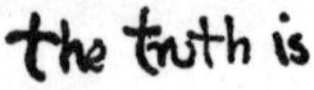

[handwritten: the truth is]

The use of the sign of the cross shows the religious person.

[handwritten: Kindness pays off]

The left slant shows the introvert.

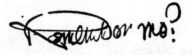

[handwritten: Remember me?]

This dramatic script belongs to an actor or actress.

CHAPTER 16

How Man Expresses Himself in Handwriting

Man has three dominant thoughts that propel him through life, that colour all he does and says and thinks, all his actions, words and thoughts.

These dominant thought processes he portrays, in many varying forms, in his handwriting.

When writing, man is completely alone with himself and with his thoughts. For the time of writing he is a recluse, cut off from the world, concentrating only on putting his thoughts and his experiences, his hopes, wishes and ambitions into words.

Whatever he has to say in his written letter, his written discourse, his essay, poems, novel or factual book, he is expressing himself in words translated from thoughts into the action of writing.

But, unknown to himself, he is also writing of his other life. The real deep-down-inside-himself-self. This he expresses in the formation of his letters and his words.

The writer is an artist. Whatever his or her station or job or position in life, the letter-writer is an artist. His paper is his canvas. His pen or pencil is his brush.

His thoughts are divided into three categories—Love, Hope, and Spirituality, and these three cover a multitude of sins.

The three primaries in painting are red, yellow and blue.

Red	Love
Yellow	Hope
Blue	Spirituality

Red—Love, covers all human emotions that are possessive, protective, sexual, sensual, sensuous.

Yellow is the sign of hope in colour psychology, whether directed to the self or to the outside world.

Blue—Spirituality, covers all emotions that are holy, religious, just, straight-dealing, intellectual, intelligent.

These emotions can be translated in terms of pictures by the artist; in music by the composer; in handwriting by the writer—by you and by me.

CHAPTER 17

Elegant — But Deceptive!

A really beautiful handwriting is pleasing to the eye. Handwriting that possesses an easy irregularity and a certain rhythm is also nice to look at. There can be a great deal of pleasure in reading a page full of neat writing or a script that consists of flowing, well-joined, uniform characters. But does everyone write beautifully, evenly, with perhaps a charming irregularity? Not so.

Invariably the forceful, go-ahead character writes with a speed and happy abandon, intent in getting thoughts down on paper as quickly as possible. The result is a scrawl or almost total illegibility.

But this is a person one can trust.

The elegant, well-formed, calculated and designed hand, the hand that is self-consciously formed—a thing of beauty to the eye—many times belongs to the vain, arrogant, overbearing personality.

So do not necessarily trust the elegant handwriter! Go more for the rough-shod writer.

Here are some specimens of pretty good handwriting that do not offend the eye. They prove how handwriting can be good, well-formed, symmetrical and rhythmical. Compare them with almost all the other specimens in this book just to prove to yourself that handwriting can look good.

But don't be mislead! The cruder, more down-to-earth specimens in this book really put humanity on stage. Rather cruelly in the spotlight perhaps. But lets face it—human nature is many-sided and it's our job to show you all those sides!

What is perfection but a bore?

Flowing, graceful, pleasing to the eye. But is the writer a pleasing personality? Probably not. Ambitious to a boring degree—overbearing and always getting tied up.

Two people can have a lot of fun!

This shows determination and an iron will. This hand exhibits a sense of power in its rhythm and flow.

One specimen is enough

Guileless and easy-on-the-eye. But such a person would be a show-off and certainly not to be depended upon in an emergency.

The curtain rose on a full house

Another example of a strong-willed individual but this can be a source of annoyance to others.

A childish mind loves nature

Soothing and restful flow. The writer would be thought benign—but here lurks sensuality.

To be or not to be – that is the question

The deliberate perfectionist who likes to have everything neatly tied up and all in its place.

The car ride was perfect

This person could be insolent, egotistical, sure of him or herself to the point of boredom.

Perhaps there is something

Dull-witted, slow thinking, ponderous.

mechanical details do not matter very much

A neat, ordered mind which likes to deal with facts.

CHAPTER 18

Signs and Symbols in Signatures

The signature is a person's very special property. It is the shape of the individual ego.

When a man or woman makes his or her signature at the end of a letter, on a document, on a cheque, in fact, on anything that is a declaration of what has just been written by them or agreed on by them, they finalise their decision or their sentiments by a flourish of line-forms that go to make the very inner essence of their particular individuality.

Here are some specimens of signatures and the types of people to whom they belong.

Vain, egotistical, conceited. The 'S' is grossly exaggerated. The dot to the 'i' is the ego.

Surrounded by a wall of inferiority. The two capital 'Cs' surround the writer with a façade of self-protection.

Strongly ambitious, a day dreamer but with great powers of visualisation and realisation. The bold cross to the 'T' denotes strong ambition, the will to 'get there'.

An artistic and creative person. Eccentric, with strong mother influence. The 'G' is pleasantly formed. The 'd' artistic in its involved strokes.

Sexually unbalanced. An emotional extremist. The grotesque 'B' is an obvious phallic symbol.

Edwards

Ambitious but lacks drive to realise all ambitions. The writing is forward but confused and hesitant in execution.

M. Reynolds

Vain, eccentric, self-centered, hypocritical. The 'M' is scrolled with affectation, the letters show self-love.

Clifton

A social climber—and likely to get there. The writer tells the world he is on the way up. The line makes a final show of power.

Janet Fisher

Precise, thrifty, prim and self-conscious. Small capitals, neat precision, each letter separate, show the neat mind.

Ivan Schultz

A dominating personality, strong-willed and vital. The writer protects himself above and below with rules that demonstrate his individuality.

Bertie Jones .

Weak-willed. A feeble personality who lacks concentration. Indecisive. Ill-formed letters show hesitancy, a weak will, a desperate attempt to justify existence.

Alfred Edwards

Lacking in confidence, with an inferiority complex. Some depression.

Frederick Merryweather

Fear of making mistakes, afraid of life.

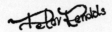

Given to exaggeration. Flamboyant. The 'P' and 'R' are rhythmic—the words have an obvious lilt.

Tries to make impressions. Not to be trusted. Another 'impressionist' striving for effect with loops and hooks.

A confused thinker, complex-ridden, a vague type. Too involved for words! Complexity and perplexity shines through all.

Powers of concentration. Continuity of thought. Decisive capitals, strong and firm, and the small letters follow through.

A defensive personality, always sure he is in the wrong. This writer surrounds himself with a fortress, encloses himself in a protective circle.

A forward-looker with drive and foresight. Speed is strongly shown. The words move on the paper.

Intense writing, neurotic with emotional inhibition. The two lines under the last word seek to justify but only stress the inbred inferiority.

Mechanically minded. Symmetrical, angular letters show the man who works out complex problems.

Sidney Oliver

An enquiring mind. Strong ego structure. The capital 'S' is a perfect question mark. This man seeks out and finds.

and an exceedingly

Immature, childish, lack of spontaneity. Slow thinker.

Eric Welsh

Sophisticated but artificial. Attempts at effect fail. The writer has not enough artistry to carry it through.

Roland Griggs

Modest personality with little drive or ambition.

Immature. Regresses to childhood. The child-ish formation of the letters speaks of immaturity and an undeveloped mind.

Strong pull from the past. The writer starts a long journey to the peak of the initial 'P' and so shows his conviction he is on the way up and will expect others to follow him.

These and many similar signatures and sets of initials can be found in every type of handwriting. It will not be a hard job to find many similar ones amongst the specimens of handwriting you are likely to come across in your search for success as a graphologist.

Extremely imaginative, warm-hearted, with sexual fantasies.

Sure of himself — the artist spirits

Energetic.

Beginning first ... start forth

Impetuous and self-centred. Doesn't think.

Hesitate. ... and all may be lost

Patronising attitude.

Bolder efforts

Ambitious, but lacks ability.

Kill-joy for ever.

Dogmatic, ruled by convention.

Voitve has its own reward

Whimsical. Good visual sense.

CHAPTER 19

The Story Told on an Envelope

When a person writes and seals an envelope with a letter inside there is an air of finality about the whole thing. The signature at the end of the letter has finalised the sentiments expressed, the ego has been projected.

Now, there remains the business of directing the missive to the right quarter so that the time and imagination spent in composing the letter, in translating thoughts into word-forms shall reach its destination and that the projection of the ego should be complete.

With these thoughts in mind the writer begins to address the envelope. With care, or with speed, whatever may be his writing habits, he writes the name and address, sticks on the stamp and seals the envelope.

Unless he is in a desperate hurry to catch the post, his mind dwells on the content of the letter while attending to the simple mechanics of addressing and sealing. His thoughts run around the things he has said. The promises he may have made, the forgiveness for which he might have asked. The good news he has imparted. The sad news he has had, regretfully, to convey.

Perhaps he has written about a personal triumph, or about hope for the future. Or, fresh from abroad, has described his travels with enthusiasm.

Whatever the case, the imaginative letter-writer invariably weaves into the envelope a sketchy pen picture of the dominant theme of the letter he has just written. And this the trained graphologist can perceive.

Beginning with basic indications, the writer of a melancholic letter will address the envelop with all lines having a decided slope that descends to the bottom right-hand corner of the envelope.

The bearer of happy news will slope his lines joyfully up from the bottom left-hand corner towards the top right-hand corner.

If the letter has contained warning news, or has described something of great importance in detail, or has been about money where the theme is on care, thrift, saving and so on, the letter-writer is likely to address the envelope bang in the middle, in a neat, careful, precise block of lines, focusing all attention, with infinite care, on the centre of the envelope.

The generous letter-writer who has offered glad hope in his letter will address his envelop in extravagant lines from side to side.

The eccentric, whose letter-content seeks to draw attention, or who is airing a grudge or grouse or laying extravagant claims will decorate his envelope with loops and twirls and scrolls.

Here are illustrations of the foregoing variations in envelope addressing.

The depressive writer.

The happy writer.

The precise, detailed writer.

The generous writer.

The eccentric writer.

The materialistic writer.

CHAPTER 20

Quick Reference Guide to Handwriting Specimens

Do something concrete about your problem

An inconsistent writer, changeable. Domesticated, but addle-brained.

Do something concrete about

Extravagant, day dreamer type. A sensual nature. An involved person.

Do something concrete about

An untidy thinker, not a planner. Musical, creative, unproductive.

Do something concrete

Emotional, neurotic.

Do Something Concrete

Weak-willed. Easily led, immature and childish.

Do something concrete

Something of a hypocrite.

Now is the time for all good men

Powerful personality but egocentric to an extreme.

Now is the time for all good men

Poor vitality.

Now is the time for all good men

Ambition-drive strongly marked. An emphatic personality.

A good, generous hand wrote this

Generosity shows in the bold, circular loops.

a mean, small-minded person penned this.

No cross to the 't' or dot to the last 'i' and the cramped hand shows the mean nature.

an emphatic person wrote this

Letters slanted both ways show a weak will.

All ambitious Scholarly person was this writer

Emotional repression.

Casually — I would never trust this

Far too exaggerated and showy. A self-conscious hand keen to make an impression. Sexual fantasies.

Uniform, rather priggish, prim and proper

Pedantic with a strong sense of pride. A difficult person.

the best thing to do is to treat this writer with care

Narrow script shows a limited range of vision.

Well-bred though a bit of a bore!

Embellished. Not very mature. Pretentious.

My dear son

This writer is eaten up with his own self-importance. He is pedantic and fatuous. He has a bad temper when roused.

and at the time

This writer is querulous, dictatorial, impulsive and petty. A hypochondriac.

Thirteen men who think

An intelligent writer with a literary mind.

Fifteen sailors went in

Vulgarity is the keynote of this hand.

please think very

Not very consistent. An unreliable sort of person.

for myself, I feel the

Strong convictions of self-righteousness. Dominating.

How people from the ends of letters is an indication of their personality.

Mean	*man*	*woman*	Thrifty
Generous	*man*	*woman*	Kind
Involved	*man*	*woman*	Clever
Pedantic	*man*	*woman*	Complex
Uncompromising	*man*	*woman*	Involved
Melancholic	*man*	*woman*	Insecure
Regressive	*man*	*woman*	Very anxious

for ever joined up

Heavy pressure shows an energetic personality with lots of vitality.

Letters Som etimes joined

An impracticable person, a slow thinker.

(handwritten: Letters linked with fluid...)

Blotted letters indicate crude sexual feelings.

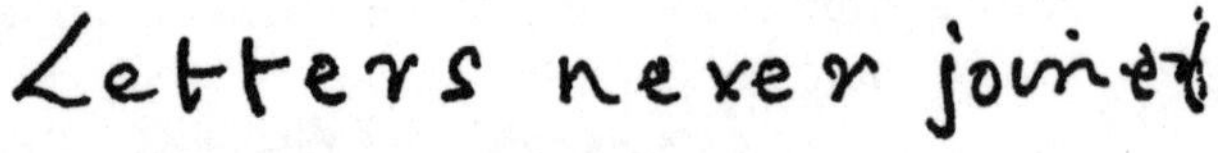

(handwritten: Letters never joined)

Immature handwriting.

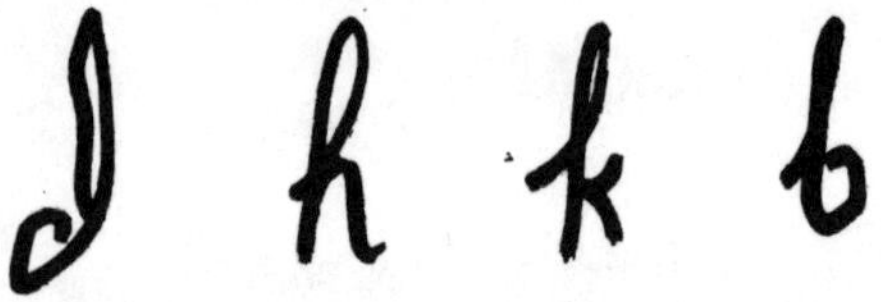

(handwritten: d h k b)

Exaggerated loops: Spiritual leanings, high aspirations.

Variations on 'd' strokes

(handwritten: d) Open ovals: a talkative person.

(handwritten: ∂) Greek 'd', a literary sign.

(handwritten: d) Tall letters indicate ambition.

(handwritten: d) Open downstroke. Argumentativeness.

PART 3

How to Read Your Own Character

CHAPTER 21

How Do You Sign Your Name?

In chapter 18, *Signs and Symbols in Signatures*, no doubt you recognised the signature nearest to that which you are in the habit of making.

This final section of this book is to help you to read and to understand your own character from your handwriting, but you should constantly refer back to the other specimen signatures and samples of handwriting to get a really clear picture of yourself.

How you sign your name is one of the most important character indications in graphology. But don't forget that if looking back on the specimens of signatures you find the one that most corresponds to your signature, and it is not a pleasant one insomuch as it does not betray a very nice character, you cannot immediately alter your character by trying to formulate a signature that looks a little more like the better type of signature in this book!

Remember also, in offering to analyse the characters of your friends, you must not ask your friends to write their names or to write anything, in fact, that is written on the spot specially for the purpose of your giving a character analysis.

Neither must you write something special, on the spot, in order to find out what sort of a character you have. It is most important that your friends give you a sample of their signature and their handwriting that has been written before you have offered to analyse their handwriting. In this way you can be sure of having an entirely unselfconscious specimen of handwriting that will betray all dominant characteristics and that will not be full of artificial whirls, curls and loops specially designed by the writer to impress you!

The same applies to you, of course. Look back on old things you have written when you start to analyse your own character. If you write things specially for the occasion you will no doubt write very carefully and try to incorporate some of the good formations you have seen in this book. Then, of course, you will have an entirely false idea of yourself.

Don't forget that the way in which you sign

your name tells your friends what sort of a person you might be even though they are not graphologists.

There is an instinctive reaction to a signature. People automatically look at a signature and try to sum up, in a simple way, the sort of person the writer of the signature is.

If you are in the habit of writing a flamboyant, exaggerated, flourishing signature, try to modify it straight away. That will not remove any characteristics you may have consistent with a flourishing, fussy signature, but at least it will hide these characteristics from others!

If, on the other hand, your signature is small, cramped and shows signs of inferior feelings and nervousness, try to put a little more boldness into it. Then people, especially those who matter most to you in life and who are likely to do you most good, will not subconsciously get the impression you are inferior!

Below, you will see an exaggerated signature and, underneath that, a simplification of the same signature, cutting out all the trimmings that betray the arrogant personality.

Below that, you will see an inferior signature and then the same signature with a little more showmanship put into it.

Examine the two sets of examples and then, looking at your signature, decide whether or not it needs a little more sparkle added to it or whether it needs to be quietened down in order to convey a better impression.

Bert Adams (signature)

Too colourful and false.

Bert Adams (signature)

Cut down a bit to give a better impression.

Bert Adams (signature)

Too small and cramped.

Bert Adams (signature)

Dressed up a little to give more power.

CHAPTER 22

How Do You Form Your Figures?

Some schoolchildren take an obvious delight in the way in which they form their figures during maths classes.

They impart to their figure work the skill and neatness of the draughtsman. The rules and lines in their cash books and exercise books are a delight to any teacher's eye.

The curves and scrolls to figures hold a fascination to these particular children and this bodes well for their future either as book-keepers, thrifty men and women or high financiers.

Other children who hate sums and dread the maths hour form their figures crudely, with many smudges and blotches; a perfect picture of a natural, in-born hatred of addition, multiplication and subtraction in general.

The adept book-keeper makes an art of figure work. Cash books are a delight to the chief cashier.

And this is precisely the way it should be. If an adult is to specialise in book-keeping as a career, is to be employed in a bank, is to look after figures in any way is, in fact, to make money out of figures, the formation of digits, their presentation and layout should be as precise and as neat as possible for the sake of maximum accuracy.

Some people write out cheques in an appalling manner. The figures are barely readable. Some housewives tot up the weekly housekeeping bills in figures that wouldn't do credit to a child. All this shows an inate hatred of the dolorous task of having to make ends meet, of the necessity for cool calculation in terms of cash. In other words, the unmathematical mind.

Bad figure work is not necessarily an indication of poor character. Of course not. Some of the genius brains of this century hate money matters, decry anything to do with cash calculations and makes no bones about being arrogantly careless with any figure work they have to do.

But, normally, one can see at a glance whether or not the man or woman would make a good business executive, good housekeeper, book-keeper, bank clerk or computer analyst.

How do you rate?

Here are some specimens of the ways in which various people form their figures and the characteristics that may be assessed from such formations.

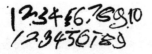

Easy money-spender. Extravagant, with little sense of values.

1234567910

Mean, mercenary, a miser-mentality.

2345676

Looks upon money as a necessary evil.

2345678

Could not care less about cash.

In figure work there is an outlet for artistic creativity. It is possible to expend loving care over the drawing of figures. For the man or woman of substance, the joy of writing down cash receipts gives an inner thrill. It is a picture of success and progress.

For the unsuccessful individual, writing figures that draw a picture of failure is a dismal task, and his attitude towards this will surely show through in the way in which he forms his figures.

How do you form your figures? Have you a successful money-mind? Or are your figures careless, slovenly undecipherable?

Only you can answer that one!

CHAPTER 23

How Do You Doodle?

Doodling is a favourite pastime of the inveterate telephone-fiend. He doodles while he waits for his contact to answer. He doodles while he talks to him. He fills every telephone notepad with his doodles. He doodles when at his office desk, working out facts and figures.

Doodles give an interesting insight into individual human nature. Doodles are the halfway-mark between straightforward writing and an attempt to draw mind-pictures. Doodles betray innermost thoughts even more graphically than does handwriting.

The doodler is sometimes an introvert, but he can also be a highly imaginative person with an active inner core of creativity 'raring to be let loose'!

Doodling is definitely a subconscious outlet for repressed and bottled-up feelings. It is the expression of the free-pen in action.

Doodlers invariably confine their doodles to a small area and get very involved with regard to pattern and design. Nine times out of ten the doodler limits himself to one continuous line that weaves an intricate pattern of thought forms. The intrinsic satisfaction gained from doodling is the making of a pattern in one continuous line that expresses the mood of the moment. It is a photograph of mind-circumstances as they obtain at the time of doodling. This is an undoubted safety-value of enormous value to the doodler. It may well be said that doodling is a temporary but habitual regression to childhood when infinite satisfaction was gained from weaving a pattern of lines into a semblance of thought-forms that expressed the child-mind.

There is a section of the mind that never grows up, and this is a mercy. For the child-mind is one that accepts simplicity and lack of responsibility. This is a useful 'mind' to which to revert from time to time when stress of living gets too much. Doodling is the ideal outlet for the child-mind in adulthood to express itself.

There follow some typical examples of doodling and an indication of the states of mind that prompted the doodles.

These do not, of course, necessarily indicate character—but they do point to character-facets that prompt the various doodle-patterns.

Squares within squares. An anxious time.

Spirals. Absorbs impressions.

Musical, artistic.

Erratic, confused.

Framed. Feels trapped.

Grille. Apprehension about the future.

Romantic. In love with love.

Compulsive urges.

Ambitious, aggressive.

Likes movement and travel.

Seeks security.

CHAPTER 24

Crosses, Dots and Loops

Crossing a 't' is a decisive action. Dotting an 'i' is a self-conscious movement of the brain and the pen.

Forming the loops of upstrokes and down-strokes is a deliberate act. Closing the letter 'o', 'a' becomes a habit-pattern. Ending letters such as 't' and 'h' and 'a'—usually when they are end letters and do not have to run-on into other letters in a word—is a gesture of finality.

When you yourself cross your 't', dot your 'i', form the upstrokes and downstrokes of your letters, close or leave open your 'o' and your 'a' and end letters such as 't' and 'h', you are subconsciously obeying habit-patterns of character that have gradually built up over the years.

Crossing your 't'

t   Slow temper. Stick in the mud.

τ   Ambitious. Progressive but could be an idealist.

f   A weak will is shown here.

ʒ   Rather an introvert. Too little attention to today.

ʈ   A forward-thinker. Plans for tomorrow.

ϵ   Easily depressed. A victim to negative suggestion.

Dotting your 'i'

ĭ   Likes to draw attention. A whimsical personality.

ì   Highly developed critical sense.

í   Sensitive, sarcastic.

ı   A strong will but rather obstinate.

í   Quick-thinking, impulsive.

ʒ   Cautious nature.

ι   Impatient, highly strung.

ι   Lacks self assurance.

Forming your loops

ʎ   Sexual resignation.

ʏ   Good judgement, fatalistic.

ʮ   Poor vitality, easily irritated.

ʒ   Energetic, imaginative and sexy.

ɥ   Will avoid responsibility, money-minded.

Closing your 'o'

o   Gossip, open, friendly.

O   A secretive sort of person.

O   Not to be trusted.

O   A cool, calculating type. Dangerous to reckon with.

O   Dishonesty and hypocrisy.

O   Discreet, can keep their own counsel.

Ending your letters 't' and 'h'

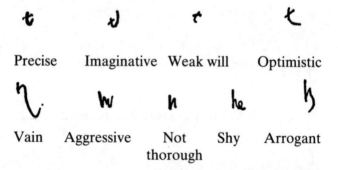

Precise	Imaginative	Weak will	Optimistic

Vain	Aggressive	Not thorough	Shy	Arrogant

CHAPTER 25

How's Your Spacing?

Do you have to write your letters on ruled paper or are you able to keep a straight line without rules?

The person who can write without rules is well-balanced in that he or she can command the eye and the hand to receive massages from the brain to keep a straight line. The inveterate ruled-paper-writer has to depend on mechanical aids to keep co-ordination of eye, brain and hand in working order. Such a person might well find difficulty in facing up to life alone, may possibly always have to have a 'prop' in some shape or form of human companionship to keep things going.

Assuming you can write without rules, how do you space out your lines of writing?

Do you keep the lines a regular distance apart, are they too far apart or do you find your lines running one into the other and experience difficulty in keeping a reasonable distance between your lines?

Lack of concentration accounts for the jammed-together lines. Lack of ability to think of what you are writing at the same time as controlling your hand and your pen. This is the sort of thing this lack of co-ordination produces.

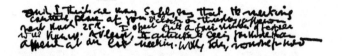

Perhaps you are over careful. Fearful of running your lines too closely together or, in fact, into each other? If so you are an over-anxious individual. You overstep the mark to make perfectly sure you are doing the right thing, but the end result is a gross exaggeration, something like this:

The party was certaining a great Success to will agree.
I am perfectly willing to hold another occasion as soon

As the left-hand margin should be quite uniform all down the left side of the page, so also should the spacing between lines be as equal as pleases the eye. Like this:

On opening the letter I was more than surprised to
find that the usual cheque was not, this time,
enclosed! I wonder if your Accounts Dept

When you write in a great hurry you may try to impress yourself that you are getting all facts down by covering a great number of sheets of notepaper by lines that are spread very wide apart.

The clear-thinker is economical in paper used; he gets his thoughts down in the quickest way possible in the smallest area possible and as clearly as possible. Like this:

Dear John,
Many thanks for writing so soon.
It really was a great joy to
hear from you as you may

The clear-thinking, well-balanced individual keeps his writing lines as even as possible, parallel with the top and the bottom of the paper, and spaces out his line equidistant. To him, the page of writing is an artistic achievement. To the tidy mind, it is a neat, centralised, uniform design. Like this:

The beginning of the evening was taken up
by introductions all round. Later, a
small presentation was made to Mrs

Lines close together show poor organising skill.

Too wide apart show the anxiety-ridden mind.

Equally spaced lines show the tidy, ordered, organised mind.

CHAPTER 26

Are You Angular?

The mechanically-minded man expresses his joy in such pursuits as mending cars, repairing electric wiring circuits and so on by insinuating into his writing sharp shapes that, subconsciously, are manifestations of what is either a loved hobby or an actual vocation.

Many of these writers (men and women) reach a certain degree of illegibility by working into their writing the hieroglyphics and signs and symbols common to their dominant interest in life.

Others, though, take as much pride in the formation of their handwriting as they do in resolving their mechanical and electrical problems. Their writing is precise, studied, a pleasure to see, highly legible but dressed, nevertheless, in the uniform of their trade.

There may be a mechanical side to your nature that you do not, at the moment, suspect. The subconscious has a funny trick of revealing itself in many little ways—not the least through handwriting. There may well be signs in your handwriting that the trained graphologist would recognise as showing potentialities in that direction.

Look at the specimens of 'mechanical' hands, noting the angular formation of the letters and words.

Hold hard to what you have in life and do not let others get the better of you. There is only one

The first specimen shows the urge for mechanical expression confused with a desire to write in a legible hand.

The experiment was completely successful in every possible way and I am happy to report that as far as I can see—

The second specimen shows the 'mechanical' artist showing through, with pride of place given to letters which illustrate the writer's rejection of curvy, artistic writing in favour of the sterner stuff of mechanisation.

CHAPTER 27

Small Writing — Small Mind?

Immediate reaction on seeing small, cramped writing is that the writer has a small, cramped mind.

This is not necessarily the case, of course, although it has been demonstrated in this book that insignificant writing can be the result of an inferiority complex or a general feeling of persecution.

Possibly you write with a small hand but would emphatically deny that you feel in the least bit inferior and certainly not persecuted!

There are, nevertheless, reasons for writing in an unusually small hand and they can be because you are confined in outlook, or unusually thrifty, or the span of your imagination is not all-embracing.

It could be, though, that you have an extraordinarily tidy and well-ordered mind and that you love to see everything in its right place at the right time. And this, quite naturally, transfers itself to your handwriting where you like to see all your letters and your words and your sentences in neat, well-ordered lines that form a pleasant pattern on your notepaper and satisfy your fetish for tidiness.

The over-houseproud housewife might well illustrate her complex in her handwriting. The cash-conscious person 'conserves' his cash in his handwriting by economising on space and laying out his correspondence in ordered lines—the 'cash book' of his mind.

The worker with a great love of detail, the genius with his infinite capacity for taking pains, the mathematician, the bank clerk, the draughtsman, the disciplinarian, the schoolteacher—such people may have a penchant for small writing. Extremely small handwriting certainly demonstrates a state of mind, often analytical and constructive.

Many men of genius, including Einstein, had minute handwriting, revealing concentration and intensity of thought.

CHAPTER 28

Sex and the Pen . . .
Male or Female?

'That looks just like a woman's handwriting' you say, taking in the graceful curves, the neat precision of the lines and the elegant capitals.

But how very wrong you can be!

You are, more likely than not, looking at the handwriting of a man whose dominant female characteristics have, as their platform, the expressive outlet of handwriting.

On the other hand, of course, you may well be looking at a woman's handwriting!

It is an accepted precept that it is difficult to determine the difference between a man's and a woman's handwritng because both sexes possess the characteristics of their opposite sex and betray and portray them in no small measure in their handwriting.

No two sets of handwriting are the same. Should not two people, (men or women) having similar characteristics, show these similar characteristics in similar ways in their handwriting, so producing handwriting that is the same? The answer to that is that certainly people with similar characteristics write those characteristics into their handwriting and so conform to the 'rules and regulations' set out for graphological analysis, but their usage and application of those similar characteristics can never be in the slightest degree perfectly similar. Therefore their interpretation of the signs and symbols will differ accordingly. The sets of handwriting can never be absolutely similar between people of predominatingly similar characteristics.

A writer, man or woman, might be vain and conceited, but one may be sensually vain, the other merely vain from a personal pride viewpoint. Both will write in an extravagant and similar fashion, but in the one the sensual theme will predominate and there will be the essential difference.

Bob Meridith

The personally vain individual

Bob Meridith

The sensually vain individual. In this second example, note the similarity between the strokes of the capitals, but here are thickened, sensual strokes that are different.

CHAPTER 29

Slope to Left or to Right?

You can be a forward-thinker or an introspective. You can plan ahead with an eagle eye on the future or you can live perpetually in the past.

You can be a day dreamer living on the memories of what has gone before or you can be a day dreamer living on hopes for the future.

You can be a constructive day dreamer—a visualiser—or you can build castles in Spain and get nowhere very quickly.

Such things naturally show in your handwriting.

If you write with a decided slope to the right, the odds are you are a concrete planner. A determined personality. A person with somewhere definite to go—most of the time.

If your writing slopes to the left, maybe you cherish dreams of yesterday too much and fail to make positive moves in the present or for the future.

And how about dead upright handwriting?

This is the sign of the ambitious personality. The higher the letters the higher the personal aims in life. The more determined the personality, the stronger the will power. And the small, condensed hand—the writing that spreads itself out across the page in elongated characters, no slope to the right or to the left and certainly not a hand that rises far above the writing line? Here is the calm, sedate, unruffled, phlegmatic individual. The cool-in-a-crisis type, the immovable, the sanguine.

Here are the styles of handwriting analysed above.

Take my advice old fellow

Slope to the right.

Take my advice old fellows

Slope to the left.

take my advice old foclos

Dead upright.

If the slant is fluctuating, it means that the person is often torn between mind and emotion. Which is your hand?

CHAPTER 30

Margins Mean So Much

The well-ordered, compact mind keeps a steady, well-aligned margin down the left-hand side of a page of writing.

It is automatic to start each new line with each letter of the first word of each new line exactly underneath the letter on the line directly above. To do this subconsciously without any effort whatsoever is the pride of the average well-ordered, disciplined man or woman.

Not to be able to line-up lines with a regular margin on the left-hand side without studied effort and deliberate scheming shows the anxiety-ridden outlook, the not-at-all-sure-of-myself attitude towards life. It demonstrates inability to grapple with the commonplace problems of everyday life.

And what about the margin on the right-hand side of the paper?

Like a skilled compositor in a printing works, the deliberate writer will so space out his words on each line that the right-hand margin ends neatly in every case on every line. But that does not mean that people who do not end their lines on the right-hand side of the paper uniformly are un-skilled, lack deliberation or anything like that. On average the typical letter writer does not line-up the right-hand margin perfectly evenly. There is usually a letter or two less, even a whole word less, at the end of lines that prevents their being completely well-aligned.

This is no failing. The dominant margin in any typed or printed piece of work is the left-hand margin and this, in most cases, is perfectly lined-up.

But such is the fluidity of thought of the hand writer that the right-hand margin is invariable ragged.

However, the writer who makes a regular habit of lining-up the right-hand margin, without fail, certainly demonstrates a very tidy, well-ordered mind and is a capable, mature person, reliable, perhaps, a little too detailed, pernickety and fastidious. He may be a mechanically-minded or extremely artistic type of individual.

The person who writes in a neat hand, well-aligned on both sides of the paper, a 'block' centralised with equal amounts of white space surrounding top, bottom and both left- and right-hand side margins paints a pen picture of complacency and loving care of and attention to detail.

Here, indeed, is the person to whom most things in life are ordered, sane patterns, who has the power to concentrate hard, to see all life as a unit of design without complexes, inhibitions or neuroses except, perhaps a compulsion for over-neatness and the desire to have everything but everything, completely cut-and-dried. Such a person would miss a great deal of the fun to be had from life, in being adventurous, taking occasional risks, forgetting to conform, from time to time, to convention and a set social pattern.

The writer who sets his script in the centre with lots of equal white space around it frames himself and his phraseology, his idea, output, philosophy and attitudes in a picture frame and tells the world 'this is me'.

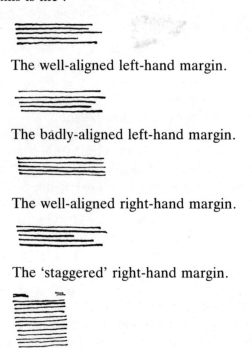

The well-aligned left-hand margin.

The badly-aligned left-hand margin.

The well-aligned right-hand margin.

The 'staggered' right-hand margin.

The centralised, framed 'block'.

CHAPTER 31

What Sort of Pen Do You Use?

In the days before the ball point pen was invented, the average lover of good handwriting enjoyed using a fountain pen. Choice of supple nibs allowed for artistry in pen strokes, especially where the signature was concerned.

Character was certainly more discernible in fountain-pen drawn letters than it is now in ball point pen drawn letters and words.

The fine, mechanical, unfeeling ball point robs writing of a great deal of character that is visible to the onlooker. But, of course, the essential formation of the handwriting is exactly the same as it is or would be were a fountain pen to be used.

But, with the fluidity and brush-smooth control of a really good fountain pen, the writer finds himself able to express himself in writing far more than is the user of a ball point pen. The sensual writer, used, by inbred habit-compulsion, to splaying out the nib of his pen when forming downstrokes and so emphasising his particular characteristics, is hard put to express himself in quite this way with a fine ball point.

To compensate, and to follow out his habit pattern, he will dig his ball point deeper into the paper, achieving a similar degree of belligerency in terms of heavier rather than thicker pen strokes. He will even go to the trouble of going over his strokes in order to get his effect.

Decorative capitals also suffer from lack of heavy, tapering up and downstrokes but, of course, the trained graphologist sees the vain, egotistical mind shining through in the midst of loops and extravagant whirls. But truly good handwriting is produced only from a fountain pen. And people who really make an art of writing always use one!

written with a ball-point pen

Not written with a ball-point pen but with a good old-fashioned fountain pen!

CHAPTER 32

Do You Write a Lot Every Day?

The more you write the better your hand may become. If you have to write a lot under pressure you are likely to develop a bad hand. But all the time, your dominant characteristics will be there and nothing will eradicate them.

Lots of people are great letter-writers. They spend hours and pages writing to relatives and friends. These people have a literary turn of mind and love the feel of a pen in their hands making impressions on white notepaper. Pen and paper are a challenge to them, as a clean canvas, paints and brushes are a challenge to the creative artist.

The person who writes a lot, whether letters, books, scripts or in the course of daily duties, is forever following a most revealing mode of self-expression, and is recording feelings and attitudes towards life.

Write as much as you can if you want to develop a good clear-cut hand. But beware of letting your thoughts run away with you. Some people write more slowly than they can think and think more quickly than they can write. The result in both cases is an illegible hand.

CHAPTER 33

Conclusion

Now . . . this is the end of the book!

You know far more now about the secrets of handwriting than you have ever known before. Possibly you have suffered a few shocks in comparing your handwriting with some of the specimens you have seen in this book. Possibly you have had your eyes opened to a few characteristics you did not suspect your friends of possessing. However, character-analysis through handwriting is an amusing pastime with its serious side when you really want to get down to the selection of friends and the rejection of foes!

As to yourself—well, by now, you will have been able to size yourself up. And the only thing to do now is to make adjustments where you think they are necessary. But don't forget—you will never change your handwriting—however much you may seek to change your character.

And that goes for all your friends and your family too!

CHAPTER 34

Glossary of Graphological Terms

(From Warren's Dictionary of Psychology)

Graphic size	Height of the short or one-space letters in handwriting.
Graphic variability	Range of variations in handwriting characteristics.
Graphokinesthetic	The muscular and other allied sensations of writing.
Graphological elements	Phases of handwriting in graphological analysis.
Graphological portrait	Interpretation of graphic signs.
Graphology	Investigation of handwriting. Personality diagnosis.
Graphomania	Obsessive desire to write.
Graphorrhea	Meaningless flow of written words.
Graphopathology	Changes in handwriting accompanying mental/physical stress.

Graphospasm	Writer's cramp. A functional spasm, an abnormal contraction or paralysis of some of the muscles used in handwriting.
Writing	Act of recording ideas in symbolic form.
Writing accent	Peculiar characteristics of a person's handwriting that appear in other persons of the same nationality.
Writing angle	Angle between the down-stroke and base-line of writing.
Writing tremor	Shaky movements from lack of muscular control.

Remember... your handwriting
is you! There is no more
true mirror to your soul
than the marks your pen
makes on paper

The Graphology Society, The Mount, Edgefield, Melton Constable, Norfolk, N24 2AE

Index